AF278351

Take Me with You, Wherever You're Going

Also by Jessica Jacobs:

Pelvis with Distance

Take Me with You, Wherever You're Going

A Memoir-in-Poems

Jessica Jacobs

Four Way Books
Tribeca

Copyright © 2019 Jessica Jacobs
No part of this book may be used or reproduced in any manner without written permission
except in the case of brief quotations embodied in critical articles and reviews.

Library of Congress Cataloging-in-Publication Data

Names: Jacobs, Jessica, 1980- author.
Title: Take me with you, wherever you're going / Jessica Jacobs.
Other titles: Take me with you, wherever you are going
Description: New York, NY : Four Way Books, 2019.
Identifiers: LCCN 2018028709 | ISBN 9781945588266 (pbk. : alk. paper)
Classification: LCC PS3610.A356433 A6 2019 | DDC 811/.6--dc23
LC record available at https://lccn.loc.gov/2018028709

This book is manufactured in the United States of America and printed on acid-free paper.

Four Way Books is a not-for-profit literary press. We are grateful for the assistance
we receive from individual donors, public arts agencies, and private foundations.

This publication is made possible with public funds from the New York State Council on the
Arts, a state agency,

We are a proud member of the Community of Literary Magazines and Presses.

To Nickole,

without you, no poems

and to Laure-Anne,

our witness, mentor, and friend

Contents

For one human to love another human being: that is perhaps the most difficult task that has been entrusted to us, the ultimate task, the final test and proof, the work for which all other work is merely preparation.

—Rainer Maria Rilke

If Marriage Means Someone Who Will Always Come Looking: A Fable

Two run through a stretch of winter, through a cold so constant there is only the myth of thaw. Hair tempered to salt-spiked quivers, eyes lashed with tears flash-frozen, veins like ice-bound rivers. Their every step, a detonation in miniature, a brume of displaced ground cloud.

They run neither from nor toward. But this is not the mystery.

One punches into a snowbank and brings forth a palmful. Though thirsty, it is offered first to the other. Cold peppers their tongues, melts

into sustenance. *Who needs to walk on water,* they ask, *when we can run on it instead, can hold it for miles in our open palms and never suffer for more?*

Yet in this cross section of bantling January, this is not the mystery.

Stalled sky-top, the noon sun rouses enough vapor to erase the day, to loose fields from their fieldness into confluence with roads.

Each counts the other's strides to stay joined in time, keeps pace with the other's breathing—*in,* two steps; *out,* two steps. But on this bleared road, how to move together and still heed the boundaries of self—still have selves at all?

In the worst of it—heavy with the miles covered, with the miles still to come—the mystery is this: They never wonder why they are there, and never wish to be anywhere else. True,

even in that expanse
of absence, in that place where, from a distance, they are two points awaiting
the thread needed to bind a button to cloth, which would in turn bind the
seam of field and sky.

When they part for a breath, running alone along the river, so that love can
follow and find, each ties red ribbons to branches—a bloodless blood trail.

If being bound as they are means they can never fully lose themselves,
then at least it also means they can never
be fully lost.

I.

I wanted to explain this life to you, even if
I had to become, over the years, someone else to do it.

—Larry Levis

Why Give an Excuse for Skinny Dipping
When You Can Tell an Origin Story Instead?

Yes, I swam naked with strangers
before we married, floated the dark coupling of creek and sky
while stars lit my skin for others, who were
not you, to see. But this was nothing
new, meant nothing;
                      as soon as I could walk, follow a trail
of shed clothes and you'd find me, mouth deep
in the lake as the rain came down, watching each drop
answered by a splash-tipped shoot:
                            for my eyes alone,
                     a fugitive garden.

Why would I let anything
      between me and that world?

                   Back on shore, backhoes
chewed hungry at the ground—today's jagged pit,
tomorrow's bulb-bordered pond. But in that
taffied summer dusk, when hours bent near
double without breaking, the hole was simply
itself: an emptiness in possession of nothing; an emptiness
to be filled with whatever I saw fit.

                 Ninety-six degrees
and one-hundred percent humidity equaled weather the same
without as within. The heat amniotic. The pit
slick with the once held breath of earth, with
runnels of mud from afternoon rain.

In a blue two-piece, I slid
the sides until my parents left and so
did the suit. New flesh on new soil,
        baptized dark by dirt. Covered that way
I was made more visible:
                        the hunger to plunge
deep enough into every moment to have my tongue
swimming in it, to learn the world with my body—a map
traced out, indelible, a map that would one day lead me to you.

Primer

A Florida child knows the safest part
of a lake is the middle. That gators
and moccasins shade in the lilies, hunker
shoreline in the muck just past
the trucked-in sand. Knows a snake egg
means a mother's nearby, and angry.
That to kill her, you must bring a shovel
down right behind her skull—leave
too much neck and the headed half will keep
coming at you. Knows to run zigzag if a gator
gives chase, their squat digger legs built
for speed, not for turning. Has a friend
who has a friend who lost a thumb
to a snapping turtle, has worn live lizards
as earrings, watched lake-caught minnows
devour a store-bought birthday
goldfish. Has been dragged on a field trip
to a sinkhole wide as a roller rink:
a red truck at the bottom, wheels up,
along with half a house and a wreck
of toys and books. Has been told it happened
on a day like any other. Has gone home
to tread water at the lake's calming
center; cool streamers of springs fluttering
her thighs, the sun a constant; the sucking
sound of a bathplug pulled, her imagination.

13th birthday and something told me to wake early

so I bellied out to the edge of our dock, fitted my fingers, palms
down, and rested my chin in their knuckled valley. Beneath
the black of the sky—a soft black, one in the process of giving itself

to morning—the water was hammered aluminum, dimpled and glossy.
But something swam against the current, surfacing at intervals: two dark peaks
visible, the terrible mouth submerged. The ruptured lake

resealed after it, while far trees charred and crumpled
as the sun rose fast behind them, its kerf of light slashing toward me,
rutting the water as a buck does a tree trunk, leaving a fragrant, bright

wound. At its touch, bass leapt, attacking minnows, each splash triggering
a band of explosions, ripples shattering against the dock.
And there I was, hovering

above a lake now boiling with fish. Me, in that body, newly a teenager,
my legs and underarms freshly clear cut, razed by razor blade, naked
to the day. Breasts heavy and foreign as a knapsack. Desire

just as weighted—an insistent pull in my gut, flush in my chest. I wanted to be
anywhere else, I wanted to be, suddenly, with
others. The brine and swell of them, the splintered smell as I lay my cheek

to the boards, new stink from my armpits, which I had not yet learned
to mask, musk from the panties I'd dreamt in—a smell I could not yet
name, the warmth of it, the sweet sour ache of a body, opening.
                                                                                          If fear

is metal in the mouth; desire, burnt sugar on the tongue; what was the taste
of that day? Of that fish-jumped, sun-stunned morning?

                                                        It was the green
of just mowed Sunday lawns, of mineral and lake muck, seaweed and algal blooms,

and, for the first time, an awareness of the taste of my own mouth, which I hoped
would one day soon taste another's. A passing plane was a silver mote
in the sky. *Take me with you, wherever you're going.*

Sex, Suddenly, Everywhere

In shop class, that redhead with the jumpsuit zippered
from throat to crotch, trilling, *Boys,*

don't touch my zipper, until they trailed her like goslings, transfixed
by the shiny metal pull. The couple caught

naked in the science building bathroom. Backhand
whispers of, *But I wouldn't even take my shoes off in there!* And how many

eighth-grade dance parties in a country club boathouse, some girl
in the corner crying about some boy, some boy nervously plucking

the wales of his corduroys, waves lapping—unheard but always lapping—
as I got freaked by the Pagan twins to a *Boys II Men* slow jam.

Confused girl meshed between two confused brothers, I tried not to stare
at the girls I wished against me instead.

∞

And every day those hallways: crowded cattle shoots, musked up
clusters of young bodies, slap of sandals, snap of bra straps, high sweet
stench of mall-bought perfume. My nose to the back of another girl's

neck, close enough to see a single strand, escaped, curling beneath
her collar, the gym class dampness between her shoulder blades. Sometimes
it was all I could do to keep my clothes on. To keep from moaning

aloud. Once a bucket—an occasional, embarrassing slosh over the top
if jostled—now a sieve, desire leaking from every pore. Which is why
I tried so hard to be harder. To use the world as my whetstone, sharpening

myself against each day. My body cried out for armor. Big boned,
broad shouldered, I was built for it: forced into a dress with shoulder pads,
I was the 90s' littlest linebacker. So I began to run, clanking

like a tank around cul-de-sacs. Began to climb, building biceps
strong enough to stiff-arm the world away. Even my heart grew
heavy, grew into one more thing to carry.

Sex Ed

Each March, the swarms arrived—my gut-wrenched
need made visible, made just as repulsive
as I'd imagined it to be: windshields caked

and rendered useless, radiators choked
with the bodies of black and red lovebugs,
kissing bugs, fuck bugs, a horror movie

façade on every building, curtains of them
unmoved by the breeze—a mob, a building
blackout. And I couldn't help

but envy them—those ardent insects, coupling
for days, even in flight—their lust
answered, each writhing creature partnered;

their desire so singular, their purpose was
obvious: they didn't even have mouths to feed.

Ain't Nothing Like Breck for Stop n' Stare Hair

It's 10 p.m. Do you know where
your children are? Well, there I was

with the remote, my thumb a die punch,
a jackhammer's relentless up and down

through a world of possible
lives—*America's Most Wanted, Nick*

at Nite, To Catch a Predator—in search
of prey worth pausing for. I slowed

though, not for shows but for
their interruptions: Bare shoulders. Wet

neck. Rope of hair glistening beneath a glistening
stream. Prell. Breck. So many ways

to get your hair glossy. So much skin
just off-screen

I tried to keep myself from wanting
to see. I rapped my wrist

with the remote; pinched the underside
of my thighs, behind

my knees—a girl's small-fingered self-
flagellation. I knew

only enough to know I should not want
this. So I called myself names, donned

shame as my hair shirt. Though I
never once turned it off. Or looked away.

And That's How I Almost Died of Foolishness in Beautiful Florida

Nights, I ran golf courses whose water traps
shone red with the eyes of alligators and rang
with their falsely innocuous chorus
of chirps. The fairway grass was less
wilderness than carpet, whispering up
its pesticides. To get home, I memorized
street signs; every house
looked the same.

                I have no doubt
that if I'd stayed—given in to the gravity
of expectations and inertia—in my push to feel
something, anything, I'd be
dead already:

              neck snapped
over the bars of a mountain bike; fallen
off a cliff while climbing; too many
drugs, the wrong kind of women, or maybe even
a husband who'd never have known why sadness
was all he brought me.

            Why I spent all day
staring at the lake, wading shoreline
where gators found their daily shade, thinking
it wouldn't be that bad, really,
couldn't be much worse than this
to offer myself to those jaws, those
daggered rows of teeth.

           Its body weighting mine
to the muck-sunk bottom, saying, *Enough
of all this air and sky. Come rest with me*

here, deep as you can. Come rest
and dream of the life you might have led
if you'd left this place, this
falsely innocuous, this beautiful Florida.

Leaving Home

The koi were killed by a possum killed by
our dog, whose barks brought my dad to the dark

yard, along with me—his stand-in son, his
midnight shadow. In the glower of the flashlight,

the dog's eyes were red and rolling, the possum's
fur bright as an errant scrap of daylight.

The dog wouldn't put it down, bent the pipe
of the pool skimmer my father used to lever

the body free from his jaws. My parents
gave the dog away soon after. Because, I suspect,

wildness can live in the suburbs only so long
as it doesn't bare its teeth; so long as when the light

finds it, it drops its prey and wags its tail;
so long as we confine our darkness to the dark.

To Florida

In the citrus light of winter, I stole oranges
from your trees; through your white sand, tore
bike tracks ragged as rope burns. In you, I was a primal thing.
                                        For years,
   I carried a keychain in your image, my name
   stamped along its length.
                    We were always claiming you,
weren't we? Your every pine
            a scarred tally of who loved whom
and when. But even before I could brush my own hair, I marched
into my parents' room and declared, *I'm not from here.*

            By *here,*
   of course, I meant *you.*
                    Though I'd never seen them, I dreamt
of mountains, of a landscape tall enough to contain me. So, yes, my first
betrayal of you was that early, that inconsolable.

                    At Ponce de León's fountain, eternal youth
had an egg-rot stink. I wouldn't drink. All I wanted was to grow old enough
to leave you.
            Florida, we never had a chance.

Empty buzzsaw of jet skis, creatures lurking the darkness
of our dock. And other darknesses, too:
            The swak of girls' thighs leaving the seat of my car. All
            the lipglossed mouths from which I couldn't look away.

Land of mowed lawns, state of near perpetual summer, in you
my longing knew no seasons. No dormancy. Eighteen years
was enough.

But my night mind grieves you. Now that I don't have to,
I come home often—for in my dreams
I just remember: swim and swim
through a day when sun columns your water
into a great hall, silt sifting like dust motes through the light; a hall
where all my earliest incarnations sit down to feast
while I skim that water's skin, calling
down to the ones I used to be.

II.

Loving is far easier than being loved. For in the first, I am in full control of the action, the transmission. What would it mean to accept something that might one day be withheld or run out? . . . What is more simultaneously freeing and enslaving?

—Alain de Botton

Why I Can't Write the Poem About How We Met

Because I came to that bar with someone else
and left with her, too. Because if it was fate,

then it's fate we fought for far too long. Because
most people who love a love story want

the streamlined when and where and how and wait
only so long for a happy ending. Because

for those six years after, I was accompanied
by a constant song—dirge of the near-miss—yet

tried to convince myself otherwise. Because
I couldn't admit I'd been wrong. Because

I didn't insist, and the time we lost is lost
for good. Because whether a story is happy

or not depends on when you end it.

What I didn't say those years you thought I'd forgotten you

was I was my own city, my own New York, and you
a succession of rolling blackouts, rolling through me
the way a shadow, each afternoon, unfurled the one ginkgo tree
on my block: a rilled eclipse,
        a dark slender bar—that mark
           of division. On the corner where 11th splits
custody between East and West, we stood
for years, a foot in either direction. The charge too much
for any wire to hold, we passed it from one to the next in a series
of cascading failures.
        Lights hushed from Houston to Battery Park.
                Dark as any July 5th
of my Florida childhood: BBQs ashed, bins
clanking with empties, Roman candles gone
to soggy paper. But once, lying alone on our dock,
I watched a meteor bisect the sky
like a thumbnail scoring the skin of a plum.
              You split me
      again and again, cast across the life
      I thought I was living.
      You swore
I'd forgotten you; I'd only wished I could.
So now, let me
      say this: Each time you returned, traffic lights failed
and pedestrians fled—the tunnels clogged as bad arteries, bridges
quivering above the glossy throat of the East River. But others,
              others stayed. Opened
    windows and kicked off sheets, made love
to battery-powered boomboxes on stoops below

where, neighbors carried grills from fire escapes to sidewalks
and shared all the food they couldn't bear to waste. Such toothsome
smells from those feasts against spoilage, those burnt
                                        offerings. And later,
                                                know there was a moment
when every office, every bar, every apartment in my city
emptied and all of us stood in the streets like the children
we'd taught ourselves not to be—hands on hips, elbows jutting
like wings, heads thrown back—remembering what had been
there all along: the night sky, suddenly visible.

Lonesome Remedy

When smudged illegible by solitude,
run the bus route, past shelter
after shelter huddled by commuters

eager for home, all turned as one
to watch for what will take them there.
Pretend it's coincidence, how you stay

just ahead of the bus, how this lands you
in their collective gaze. A moving
object from the right direction—their eyes

can't help but find you. Don't stop.
Simply to be seen is a kind of salvation.
Run through their longing. Pretend

you are what they've been waiting for.
Run. Pretend such pretending is enough.

In New York, I Remember Greece
(So as Not to Remember Her)

Blind sentries of skyscrapers, blind centuries of bedrock,
don't mind me—this blip biking down Broadway
through the warm summer rain, trying to think of anything
but the vivisection of my days
                      into before, during, and the inevitable
              after, which morphs into just another
before—the countdown that resets itself
                                      each time she walks away.

Shush of taxi tires, sweet acrid scent
of the road opening itself to the weather, a scent
Greeked by some geek into *petrichor*—
petra, the word for stone, and *ichor,* the holy
consommé that broths the veins of gods
instead of blood. So perhaps

                  memories of Naxos instead, that island I fled to
at twenty-two with my impractical degree, mixing drinks
for already drunk Brits and Swedes. An island known best
                              for the Portara—
a massive ruined door from the finest temple
never built, once connected
to the mainland but now standing
on its own little island, the water around it rising.
                                      A door from
and to nothing, nowhere.
                      And now?
                                      In the right light,
a portal perhaps, an invitation to imagine. Which I did

each day before my shift, pedaling a battered push-bike
into the mountains and, after work, tipsy
off the dregs of cocktail shakers, while swimming
naked in the night sea.
>What did it say about me
>that the most romantic trip of my life
>was one I took alone?

I squinted through three months of postcard-perfect
sand-and-surf until the single day it finally
rained, rendering all the days before it
two-dimensional, without contrast or perspective.

I walked the ancient part
of the city, where streets labyrinthed
into narrow alleys meant to confound invaders,
the too-high-to-see-over walls a highway for feral
cats stalking octopus tentacles
clipped to dry on laundry lines.

A dim doorway, an old man
leaning on a cane over a young man
crouched against the jamb, his hands
cupped around a cigarette.

What is wrong with you? the old man asked
as the young man struggled with his lighter.
My heart hurts.
Prodding him with his cane, he asked,

Why don't you go to the doctor?
        The young man looked up.
       He cannot understand this pain.

And that's where, in memory at least,
                      that day ends, leaving me
here, on another island,
      on this Manhattan avenue wide enough to welcome
every invader; alone
    with the same smell of rain, with an ache
        doctors have no chance of curing.

Postcards Braver Than I Could Be

unsent, year after year

∞

The week you spent in New York took my city and renamed all the streets, designated a new set of landmarks.

∞

13th and 5th—Your look there asked, *Is it you? If you are the one, if I require saving, would you, could you do it?*

∞

West 11th and 6th—A small Jewish cemetery, tucked behind a peeling black gate. You brought me to the bars, had me peer in. A street I'd run a hundred times, just like that, made new.

∞

East 11th and Broadway—My apartment, now little more than the site of your gray scarf's endless unwinding. Of your throat, finally bare. Of the weight of your breasts in my palms as you straddled my hips. The place I fled to run after you, out into the street, but you'd already left.

∞

Memory as film reel—each image lost to the next so swiftly my eyes lie to conjure broken moments whole. Flash them past fast enough and there you are again in my arms.

To a Florida Girl, Spring Was Just a Poetic Convention

Having known only Florida's poor translation
of seasons—summer/not-summer—
I flunked my first exam

at a northern college, unable to link *primavera*
to its months; I could name all twelve in Spanish
but couldn't answer that question

in English. Then I survived my first winter
and watched the world return
to color. Girls sunbathed on grass

still cornered by snowdrifts. Who cared that goosebumps
made them a quad-full of chickens
plucked for the pot? After a season of overcoats,

they were so much sudden skin. All of it
a lesson, really, in the value of denial, in how
the delay of gratification can make it, later,

all the more gratifying.
                    Like that one
ice-choked morning in March—nearly twenty years

after my first real spring, six years
after first learning your name—we sat together
in a conference hall, amid aisle after aisle

of unturned pages, and began the conversation
that became our marriage. And when I cradled
your jaw in my palm, I had one thought:

So this is how it finally begins. Spring
for the person who never believed in it.

III.

Whatever shadow there was in that world
it was the one each cast
onto the other,
the thin black seam
they seemed to be trying to work away
between them.

—Jorie Graham

Out of the Windfields

When combines brought the fields
to their knees, it felt like running

an arid spreadsheet. Grid by grid,
I logged my miles, the hours

on my feet, but kept true account of nothing
so much as my loneliness. How long

since I'd been held there,
even by water, given my weight to another?

All winter, the sky was desolate
white of a mussel's middle leeched by cold

of its gasoline glimmer. Static
landscape, untongued by tides. Yet constant

as lighthouses were the turbines. Idle,
they were sky-flung starfish

far from the sea, but moving they were
majestic, amphibious animals in their proper

element. Able to arc into the unseeable and return
with power. I tried to do the same.

But instead was desiccated, field-stripped, brittled
down to parts. Then there you were. Beside me

as my headlights slid the storm-slick streets. Submerged
together, a turbine's red light pulsing its beacon

through the rain. Beneath it, your hands
bound me back together. In answering

prayer, I folded myself into the footwell; knelt
between your knees. And

my mouth to you was every water
I'd ever tasted: clean shock

of snowmelt in an alpine pond; tongue cased
in ocean's wetsuit of salt; green and mineral

of a springfed lake—but most of all,
chlorine's high bite in the throatback

of every Florida pool in summer, the water
so bath-warm, so body-kindred, that entering

was like sliding into another skin—skin
that entered you back.

Thanks, stupid heart

like for that time I'd banished her
number from every device I owned
only to find the digits scrawled on your
anterior wall. *Diastole*, you whispered,

relax and fill. But what did you know?
Flushing and pumping like a jellyfish
going nowhere, stuffed between my lungs'
pink wings like an ugly flightless bird.

The trick pony of my brain was ready
to wander other pastures, wonder other
futures, but you—grown from the same stock
as *courage* and *accord*—she was your only

aim, and faithful dumb muscle you are, stupid
beautiful heart, you beat only for her.

When your surgeon brought snapshots
to the waiting room

your body was still a new thing to me. And here
                         was your right ovary,
ash gray and threatening rain, brindled by firebrick veins. Fat, a cluster
of discarded yolks. And your uterus, an unblossomed pink
peony, crawling with fibroids invasive
but benign as a swarm of white ants. This was not the garden
you'd abandoned in Kentucky for a patch
of dry Arkansas earth—certainly not
the garden you wanted *us* to grow.
                         Somewhere, off-screen,
your heart's fist performed its steady squeeze and release, just
as my hands had in my lap since you were wheeled away, as they had
by my side while pacing between chairs bolted to the floor, had all along
the scuffed anonymous halls.

        When they finally let me back, I wanted to report
that inside you I'd seen a vision of a vast cathedral, or one of those
underground cities, complete with chapels and wineries.
But, really, what I saw
                         was a small apartment in a bad neighborhood,
the one lent to us by a friend for that month
of your recovery.
                         Its air tanged by new
paint. Its kitchen housing no more and no less
than two bowls, two plates, two forks, two spoons. Our
bedside tables, overturned bins; our first shared bed
an inflatable with a slow leak, where—despite your pain, despite
your nausea—we managed to find each other. Where
before sleep, we'd watch sitcoms on a phone

propped against my thighs: tiny figures living out tiny lives
on a screen smaller than a pack of cards, in homes
far better provisioned than ours; though watching them,
in their many rooms (stale air whispering
from the mattress, our backs growing closer
to the floor); I couldn't see a single thing I wanted
                                        more than this.

Post-op, still out of it, you said, *I would*

you know, if we aren't jerks, I'd marry you.
We'd known each other, in that moment, years
yet spent fewer than two weeks together. *You fill my heart with koi
and dahlias,* you said, which took me
                                        back to the backyard pond
my dad mucked out each weekend, pumps clogged with
lake silt and clam shells, water brown as a drainage ditch.
                                        But the koi
persisted, bright as still-wrapped birthday gifts. The emissaries
of better places.

        Like later, when we visited that Big Sur inn, red dahlias
out front broad as the plates from which we ate barbecue
to bursting. Each floret a deeper red at its center
                        —How many states have we passed through?
How many miles have we driven?
        *Since we're not young, weeks have to do time
        for years of missing each other—*
                                or like that painter's studio
in Taos with his triptych the yellow-gold of the dahlias
you'd envisioned, koi swimming the canvas; your dream made
manifest, sunset pouring past the mountains
to deepen the tones.
                Past midnight, we drove back down to Santa Fe.
Along the high desert road, the city lights ahead
were a grounded planetarium, abundant as the lightning
bugs we saw barber-poling every grass blade
in Tennessee.

That having you
                    as my witness would make of this life a shared
palimpsest—the already lived
life still shining through, would make our past into a series
of parallel presents, I couldn't have known, but sensed somehow.
                                        Which is why, even in those early days,
in the whiteness of that hospital bathroom, the one I'd nearly had to carry you
to, the one whose white tiles were so bright it was as though our eyes
were closed and it was not the tiles we saw
but their after-image—a brightness of which you, with your wan face
and alabaster arms, were a part—when your pelvis tipped
to ribbon your inner thigh with blood, I could do nothing but
                        comfort you and clean you as if
you were my own. Because you were, even then.

Laying Down the Veils

Poised is the word most applied by others—you
who makes even a sweatshirt look classy,
who always knows just what to say. But

for me, nearly knowing you is nowhere
near enough; so know this: on your right knee, I love
these forgotten bristles. Your holdover pronunciations

that oomph *voluptuous* into *volumptous*
or ask, Why *thaw* a frozen chicken breast
when you can *dethaw* it instead?

Each fallen fantasy,
for me, another fact to keep. The near
endless time you take before

a bathroom mirror, before deciding
anything, or finding all those right words
to say. The sags and wrinkles I hope to be

around to see. And most of all, how you
know me too—my clutter and sweat, my need
for now instead of later, how I cry

during the rousing speeches
in action movies, how my gentleness
is more learned than given—that you

know all this and love me still.
Ignored, any difficulty can become
the small thing that is

the only thing, the lichen that shears
the mountain in two. So the world
can have the airbrushed models, faces

firmly in place. Here, the mystery
is dead, long live the mystery.

Postcards, After the Fall

from a defunct fiber farm in Western Massachusetts

∞

The animals of Eden have grown old. Beneath swayback spines, the sides of their bellies almost touch. The camel's fur is clumped with dung and bits of hay and, one day, the second emu just lies down and dies. The donkeys bray like sirens. One sheep's rear legs barely bend; its hooves drag the concrete pen, sending up no sparks. For a blade of grass, a peacock displays himself.

∞

The poet who owns this place steers the stead from her kitchen table. She wakes early, before the world comes calling, to prop her elbows there and divine from coffee grounds her lapsarian lines. Who needs Adam? Who needs Eve? There is paradise enough here for the rest of us.

∞

Crows declare from the bare branches of the beech trees, leaving the leafed boughs for birds weak enough to need that shelter.

∞

Each morning, the emu peers through our window: deep amber eyes above a blunted black beak, thin neck plucked to bare blue skin, his body is a cross between an ostrich, an umbrella, and a disheveled epaulet. His feet are massive, blackened and leathery with dagger-sharp claws and thick meaty pads. A vestigial talon crowns each wingtip, commemorating dinosaur days. Fluffy pterodactyl, he eats the peach slices my wife offers while I watch from behind the lattice. When she has no more, he pecks the top of her head. His thin feathers gleam.

∞

Along the chipseal lane, tiger lilies slum among ditch weeds. Nothing goes to waste here: teasel pods are dried to card the wool, empty feedbags store the winter tinder, and scrub grass is converted to milk and meat.

∞

In the daylight, we drag our mattress to the hallway, the only place in our room without windows. Endless gratitude for the press of her thighs to my sides, for her warm weight, for the sky shining in, her eyes met by the blue at her back.

∞

Even once all the grass is gone, the camel's lips are gentle and searching on my palm. He lets me pet his throat as though he's beginning to trust me.

∞

Two pygmy donkeys—we call them the Balthazars—scratch their tired necks against trees bent from years of that service.

∞

To be happy, the poet farmer says, *an animal must have another of its kind.* Goat with goat, donkeys together. And, without a mate, the lone horse makes due with the camel. They graze together in adjacent enclosures; when one is called to the barn to eat, the other races inside to keep watch, staring over the fence that divides them.

∞

In the sheep's paddock, we lie in the grass. She traces a message across my skin. *Now your shoulder knows something the rest of you doesn't.*

∞

The camel's softest place is the warm valley behind his jaw. Around each eye, a muff of spiky, sun-bleached fur. This farm is strange enough to make us, within it, children again, the world new and full of wonder.

∞

Bravo, brave Maremma sheepdog, white wonder who noons in a pit dug beneath the picnic table and sleeps nights outside the front door, is this farm's protector. He chases bears from the cherry trees, yet presses his head to my knees when it thunders.

∞

We have fought, falling into argument like we too often do, fast and with nothing much behind it. She calls me outside to the folding green chairs, to the charged night air. Sits in my lap in apology, points to the sky. The heat lightning is silent, without companionable thunder. Bravo's fur flashes back its own bolts. The whole sky is a child's night light, a midnight mountain storm globe. She brings my reluctant head to her chest, wraps my arms around her.

∞

On farms, you learn to leave gates as you found them. What is penned must stay penned; the so many things that must be kept out, kept out. Is marriage any different? Yet we've vowed to be not just honest but forthright, to leave every gate open. No wonder this is difficult.

When You Ask Me Why We Took So Long

I could tell you
again how tired I was then, how
disillusioned. The real answer,
though? I have no idea. But I do know
this:

Even with evidence
of recent rain, a desert
says only dryness. Its low bushes brittle,
its cracked earth red as rust.

Yet this hides the land's precocity
for flooding.
For after weeks, sometimes
months, of empty skies, when
rain finally arrives,
it's repelled.

No matter how thirsty
the ground, after so long
without water, it has forgotten
how to drink.

Who Needs Premarital Counseling When We Have Nightly Visits to the Doubt Couch?

in a borrowed cabin in Michigan's Upper Peninsula

On the loveseat meant for one
and a half, we are a snake's nest
of limbs—not comfortable
but in love. We begin:

> *children money religion sex*
> *Tell me your flaws* (a test
> of self-awareness). *Now, tell me*
> *mine* (a test of attention, of how honest
> or stupid you're willing to be).
> *And what do you love*
> *in me?* (translation: Does your love
> match the little corner I love
> in myself?)

Outside and only a mile away,
the Devil's Slide: a groove
once used to skid logs
to barges waiting on the lake, so steep
the ground caught fire
with their speed. Now a tourist trap
where you ditch your shoes
to whoop and holler and surf the sand
five-hundred feet down, taking care
to watch for the hidden rocks
that can send you ass over teakettle
all the way to the bottom. Climbing

50

back up, however, is another matter;
an arduous plod with much
backsliding, much cursing
and catching of breath and craning
of head to assure the top
is still there and, yes,
you will one day reach it. Much swearing
that you will never again, ever—
though you will and you do. Each night,
our every question, the same.

Elopement Epithalamium

October 21-22, 2013:
Santa Barbara→Little Rock

Because the day after we married
we were scheduled to teach, our wedding night
was pretzels and hummus from a plastic cup,
cut fruit, and a midnight flight. A Boeing cabin
was our marital chamber, with all the standard humiliations
of a plane: snaky whisper from the overhead vent, seatback pockets
sticky as a kangaroo's pouch, and the complaining bowels
of strangers, none of whom knew or cared
we were newlyweds—recognition of our marriage dependent,
anyway, on which state we were flying over. That
and all the crying babies. And row after row
of inflatable neck pillows.
                            But around her neck—my wife's
neck—a scarf the goldenrod yellow of deep joy. Opened,
it blanketed us both. We pulled up the hoods
of our sweatshirts and I took her left hand
in mine. No party, no speeches, no gifts;
beneath the cabin's din, just our simple silver rings
together, sending up their small chimes.
With her head on my shoulder, she slept,
                            while I repeated,
silently, our vows, the ones we'd struggled over
many nights in bed: *Why a semi-colon*
when a comma might do? Can we focus more
on promises than prohibitions? This was how
two poets learned to share. This, why

we'd needed to marry
as we did, without distraction
of seating orders or centerpieces. We had enough
appliances. No longer children, we knew
               what we were getting into. Each of us
holding the hand of the most
stubborn person we knew, the only one capable
            of wrenching the other
greater than the sum of her parts.
                    And so, awake and watching every moment
              of that flight, I can say with certainty
                we departed one day, landed in another,
      and disembarked in another state entirely.

A Question to Ask Once the Honeymoon Is Over

Big around as my bike helmet and high as my ankle, the box turtle
was halfway from my side of the road
to the other. The warm sun felt delicious;
my legs, strong, and it was almost
to the center line. I hadn't been passed by a car
for miles. Figuring if it was still there, I'd pick it up
on the way back, I cycled past.

                                              Years before,
the woman across the street was shaped like that turtle,
or more like a toadstool, really, squat bell
of a body atop the thin stalks of her legs, milky and bare
beneath her frayed black housedress. It hurt her to move—clear
even from my second-story window—so she brought
her trash out in increments, in small, bursting
grocery bags. She tossed each out the door onto the porch, then
nudged them, one step to the next, before easing—carefully,
painfully—herself down, a step at a time. Then she toed them,
finally, slowly, slowly into a crumpled heap at the curb. I left
my window to help; then took her trash out every week after.
                                    That story—
                          I hadn't yet
                                        told it to my wife, had I?

                    But there was the turnaround
quicker than expected and I spun
to find a beat-down bus trailed by all the fuming cars
that hadn't passed me.

Steadying my handlebars against the wind,
I rode back hard, dodging around crushed
squirrels and tire-splayed birds.
                              The turtle
was just where I'd left it, but with the top of its shell
torn away. The dead turtle,
a raw red bowl, its blood slashing the twinned yellow lines
into an unequal sign,
              as in a ≠ b, as in thinking about doing the right thing
is not the same as doing it. As in, how many times
did I watch that old woman shuffle bags down the stairs
(*really, how many?*) before I went from watching
to helping? As in, with my wife beside me
I am the woman who does not hesitate
to lay down her bike and give a small life
safe passage. As in, I biked slowly
home, told no one. As in:

        Will she love me
            less when she learns
        I am not equal
                    to the person I am when she is watching?

IV.

It is leviathan and we
in its belly
looking for joy, some joy
not to be known outside it

two by two in the ark of
the ache of it.

—Denise Levertov, "The Ache of Marriage"

Though we made love in the afternoons

Santa Fe, NM

we fought each night in the smallness of our rented room, escaping
into mornings shocked and squalled by two magpies
protecting a hidden nest. *Desert penguins*, we called them—
larger than jays, smaller than ravens—those words
                                        not quite right,
                        certainly not enough,
but to describe a thing not yet known,
comparison is sometimes the closest we can get.

    Like a year earlier,
hobbling through our first
ever weeks apart—you, in Arkansas; I, in Montana—lovesick
as teenagers—the only place with reception
was a field drowsed at dusk by bees. I stood for hours
amid their slow circling, still as I could, so your voice could find me.
                        There, in someone else's mountain homestead,
another nest. Tucked in a crook, it held four newly hatched
robins, their beaks white as the insides of orange rinds; bodies
like muscles stripped of skin, twists of gray-red flexing. Their heads—
awkward pincushions, mohawked—lolled
the twig walls, eyes sealed, mouths gaping. Below,
a girl with hair streaked pink (she emphasized the "and-a-half"
when she told me her age) swung in a hammock
looped from their tree to a shattered-glass greenhouse.
                                        Because she
already existed, she was more than the child we
imagined, but less, too, in that she was blemished by being
not ours.

Just as the years we weren't yet together were both
better and worse than those ahead when one of us
will die while the other must stay and remember. Better
in that we did not yet know that magnitude of loss; worse,
in that we did not yet know what we would one day have
to lose. Yet, still we bicker about nothing
and risk everything. Let us instead
be those fledglings, those new things. Be
that thin-ribbed nest of four-chambered need: Let us
guard and soothe and feed. Accept the other's
imperfections—and our own—as just the right type
of decay. Please, say you'll stay with me
until nothing is finished, until we weather
beyond measure of words.

In a Thicket of Body-Bent Grass

Arkansas is aspic with last-gasp summer, making running
like tunneling: the trail's air a gelatin
of trapped trajectories.

                  Yet deer float the twilight field,
ears periscoping the woody browse.
       While bucks bed alone
in deadfall and ditches, trusting themselves
to thick cover, females gather
              where wind can breathe in
a predator's scent. Forelegs origamied into a mantis prayer,
they are poised to spring even when sleeping,
survival a balance between stillness and startle.

                       I stop, kneel, stalk
along blowdown of sumac and hackberry, cowlicks of crab grass.
Eye level, the field is messy as a made bed unmade
by love, my hands greened and musked
from ungulate scat and piss. The deer—dark hillocks merged
with their shadows—welcome the animal
                    I've become, offer
an abandoned bed, matted and dusky as the sweated twists
at the base of your head those mornings you wake to thank
death for conceding another day. For the slatted light bugling
through the shades. For my palms to your breasts, my breath
to your neck.
        Here, though,
            tonight, creature
in another creature's bed, I am taking

just a moment to be an animal alone
in my own head. All while you, I know, are home,
trying not to look for me, again,
out a window grown so dark it just reflects.

Forgive me. I'd grown so used to being lonely.

In the First Fall of Our Marriage

Though I want to give you
only kindness, there's often an age between what I want
                                     and who I am.
Yet how many times can you cry on my chest before something
good grows there?
                 Redwoods thrive in acid soil; summon
that weight, those stiff-fingered roots
to skewer my ribs and prime the rusted pump
in my chest. Into that age, let me
                           grow: a ring for each year, marking
boom and drought and flood. Let me anchor further, into
your roots; make me part of something
greater. Let me grow strong enough
that even when fallen
        I can be of use to you—
                           rough lumber for rafters and joists, a roof
for the drum of this evening's insistent rain. A cross-section
from my trunk set to spin on the phonograph—a record
of what has passed, playing the music of what
is to come. A song for each year
        I'll learn to love you better.

Curly, My Tangler

Other lovers want to live with particular eyes
I only want to be your stylist.
                    —Pablo Neruda

Who needs Rumpelstiltskin, when such treasure
abounds: her gold woven

around my bike gears, tangled in my toothbrush,
vining every drain—even, sometimes, found

in my mouth upon waking. And just
this morning, from the bathroom, she called me in.
          My mama's the only one who ever
          brushed out my hair, she said. *But you're*
          my wife. You should know.

I began at the bottom, her curls separating
with the thick sound of good cloth tearing.
          Do you see why I had no friends
          when I was little? she asked. *Mama*
          brushed out my hair each day before school.

I eased my fingers, for the first time,
all the way through; asked how that felt for her.
          Vulnerable, she said.

Shimmering out beneath the overhead light—a climbing
of kudzu, a symphony of trumpet vines—her hair revealed itself.

It was like Velcro, she said. *Anything would stick in it—*
bubble gum, spitwads, pencils. I'd come home crying
and Mama would hold my ugly, frizzy head
and say, Baby, they're just jealous.
As though her love could make the lie so.

When it comes to her, her mother and I
have this kind of love in common. Only now, the lie

has come to pass. My wife, whose hair
is the shade of farm-fresh yolks, the color of things rich

on the tongue. Whose hair sings the plaintive song
of bed springs. Whose hair is the drifting

smoke from a village of chimneys, corkscrews
enough for a thousand bottles of wine. A ski slope

of s-curves, a grove of twirling maple keys,
every playground slide

worth sliding. Before a rapt audience,
a company of ballerinas cambers their hands

to trace out, in the air, your hair; my dear angora
goat, my cloud of bats spiraling from the cave.

Your mouth to me

is like after a long run, when I ease
my tiredness into a hot bath

just like we slide the dishes
of an into-the-small-hours

dinner party into a brimming sink
to soak. Slick husk of sweat

loosed like the kiss of oil from a pan—
each freed drop, a small gold world

ascending the dark water
to galaxy the soap suds. My body

in that bath rhythmed
by its currents—blood and

breath—until I can give myself
to the release

of stillness, eyes closed,
ascending, unmoored from my bones.

When You Ask About My Tramp Years

A detail, a gesture—
how one spoke in accents when nervous, how another kissed
my knuckles every morning upon waking—
                                    can be followed
        like a thread through the labyrinth
                    to a scene, a moment shared
        with one of the ones I loved
                            before I loved you.

                                            From them
I learned comic timing, appreciation of sculpture, kindness,
culture, and, from the first, that I too could be crushed
by the unrequited.

                But so what
                    if their tics accreted
like barnacles; so what if I'm coral—a small-beings collective
masquerading as indivisible whole?
                                If I am, then so
        are you: the dirty rock star, the impetuous
artist, that kind boy who sold his car
to buy you a ring.
                Each of us,
a tapestry rough with foreign fibers; each
with others layered like glass across our vision, fine-ground
into the lenses through which we see.

                        But sometimes
                        when you have me press

my lips to yours until it hurts, is it because you, too, want each kiss
to remake you? To change you back
into that uncivilized, original place
      where there are no footsteps
                but mine?

                    For if I can do it,
                        so can you,

        by the goad of our jealousy,
                each of us made new.

Between the Shoreline and the Sea

Shards of beer bottles are back-and-forthed into something
beautiful. With a clicking pocketful, we walked

Provincetown's breakwater where a woman handed us rosehips,
urging, "Sailors ate them against scurvy," their burnt

red skin taut and tart on the tongue. To thank her,
you said, *It's not every day*

I get to do something for the first time. But the very next morning,
there we were, half-asleep, on the lowtide beach for our first

shared daybreak. The night before—can you even remember
what we fought about? Every argument leaves me

closed and fighting my way back to you.
So beside the metal retaining wall, I held you beneath

a set of slippery stairs, the wall's elaborate rust
its own sunrise. Across the bay, the shore was sheathed

by only a skim of ocean, busied by beach combers. And every
one of them kept their eyes down. Chose against the new sun

to look instead for bivalves—oysters, mussels, clams—
small things that open completely

only when they die. Earlier though, do you remember?
From your sleep, you murmured, *I love the robin*

you put in my chest. It's just a common little bird but it's so sweet and it sings. Oh, to have something singing

inside us, our bodies homes for such joy. To accept strange gifts and believe the unknown we take in

will be enough to save us.

In the Grove of Self-Charging Trees

Darling do you remember
the [one] you married? Touch me,
remind me who I am.
　　　　—Stanley Kunitz

It is early enough that fog still skeins
　　the highest branches.
And twining each tree: a cable
rough-creped as wild grape vine,
with both ends socketed
into the trunk. Murmur and fizz
of power pulled from the sky,
　　　　from the earth—power recirculated
by the cables, nothing wasted.
　　　　　　　　　　In a clearing
no bigger than our cabin's double bed, you spread
a blue blanket. We make a picnic
of a peach and a plum. Then, with no top sheet, no
clothes, not even a bracelet—How long has it been,
　　　　love, since we touched? Even
　　　　　　our kisses are given
　　　　　　　　　　on the way to something else.
　　　　Yet here, our bodies
do not just tighten but seal
fast around the other and we
kiss the kind of kiss that's like entering
a glass cathedral, a structure that exists
to emphasize the space it contains
while leaving visible all it does not.

We move
        into that kiss as we move
into each other—with gentle
        force, a matched insistence—
and all the trees begin to hum. Self-charging circuits,
all of us, drawing from the world
      a stream of heat and light, which we pass between us
   like a fire that burns but does not consume.

          I wake to your back; your body
an early-morning house in which all the inhabitants are still
asleep, the lights extinguished, the doors locked and bolted. Yet
      beside our bed, the marigolds you brought me
burn like paper caught in the act of ignition, orange and red
petals of flame. And on each of our ring-fingers, the same
silver band: my promise to you,
   my charge, that through the forest and fog, through
the busy thicket, I will
never stop finding my way
       to your door. All I need from you
   is to answer;
     all you have to do is let me in.

In Wyoming

All the flies in the valley were buzzing at the windows, wingflits
fizzing the afternoon bright as sparkling water. As they
were our only neighbors, we climbed the loft's ladder clothed
and descended it naked, proud not to have clocked our heads
against the roof's crossbeam, woozy nonetheless
with that suspended, elevated hour. An hour when we
almost, just nearly slipped our skins, lost track
of our insistent edges. That good kind of losing.

If our cabin were the barn next door, this loft would be
where the hay was stored—bale after bale of sun-drenched stalks,
the herds feasting all winter on summer.

I've returned now alone, to read, but mostly
to listen, hovering in the god-seat:
There's the loose flutter of a mare's sigh, half-asleep
in the yard. Above, the teeth-on-tin screech of a hawk; below
the tink of her spoon on a dish as she scoops up peas cooked
slow with butter and salt, as she was taught as a child, a helping
of home in these faraway mountains.

Up here, unseen, the heat
drifts up from the stove's glow, the peas' haze, my love's
contented breath, the memory of her face beneath mine—
simmering

until I am blanched as a boiled tomato and a single touch
is all it would take to part my skin in a neat seam, a touch
to peel back this pored, porous facade so I can drift down and
settle inside her like steam. Like whatever comfort and ripeness
                                              her body might need.

My Winded Love, My Sweet Shuffler

∞

When, on this looped trail,
she scuffles left (trying, always trying) and I run
right, it means running both
                              away from and back toward
her. Disappearance and return:
A way to practice death; a daily way
to experience resurrection.

∞

Without a shirt, air eddies my ribcage. Without a watch,
no cultured clock time. Just poplars casting their long lines
of shadow, swallows ceding bats the sky. Without shoes,
the damp earth eases up to meet me, my steps quiet enough
the deer only quiver at my sudden scent—one, a fawn so young
its flanks are still licked dark by its mother's tongue.

                              Earlier,
beneath our cool blue sheets, when I brought my mouth to her
before her eyes had even opened, she
                    said, *In my dream, you were*
inside me. Did you know it? Were you there, too?

∞

In these woods, winter is a brown room, and here we are, inside it
together. Above, the sky is stained glass cut by a leading
of brown branches. Between the trunks, a thousand blue doors.
We are in need of no keys. The light is on

75

the river where gulls rise like ashes
of the sun's setting
fire.
    Does she see it, too?
                My eyes strain
around each corner, ears hunt
her returning step.

∞

No matter how many times
this running apart
to come back to each other
works, there's always a moment I'm sure
I've lost her. A moment my head goes
dark.
      But between the birches, there
she is, high-stepping
up a hill, panting a bit, yelling
my name, flushed, and happy.

                We
are on the forest's far side. This day, well
on its way to the next.
              Whether it's hers
or mine, with a shared pace, a shared
          direction, let us turn and return
    as one, continuing on
   together in whatever light
              is left to us.

Stridulation Sonnet

Tiger beetles, crickets, velvet ants, all
know the useful friction of part on part,
how rub of wing to leg, plectrum to file,
marks territories, summons mates. How

a lip rasped over finely tined ridges can
play sweet as a needle on vinyl. But
sometimes a lone body is not enough.
So a sapsucker drums the chimney flash

for our amped-up morning reveille. Or,
later, home again, the wind's papery
come hither through the locust leaves. The roof
arcing its tin back to meet the rain.

The bed's soft creak as I roll to my side.
What sounds will your body make against mine?

Kina Hora

We measure our days in honey, you say, *a bottle a week, then back
to the grocery*, tipping the last of this one into not your cup
but mine. My Jewish upbringing demands I be frightened
of such uncomplicated happiness.

         When I was a kid and got something stuck
in my eye, my grandmother's solution was to hold open the lid
with thumb and forefinger and say, *pu-pu-pu*. I laughed but did it,
I laughed but it worked every time. It was only later
                         I learned it was an antidote
to *ayin hara*, the evil eye—that hex golemed up by a neighbor's envious
ogle, or, if you got too uppity, it was God's
wrathful gaze swatting you back to size.
                             *Sefer Chasidim, The Book
of the Pious*, notes, *One should not believe in superstitions*. Yet, even it
cannot help adding, in a pinch of salt over its literary shoulder, *But it is best
to be heedful of them*. Thus was I schooled
                    in the positive value
                of negative thinking.

         So when you sit at the kitchen table—*our* kitchen table,
writing a new poem, when my legs carry me
miles up a mountain trail, when I return
to your serious face still bound to the page, when your face's weather
lifts at the sight of me, I wish
               for every anti-evil blue-eye amulet
hawked in Istanbul's Grand Bazaar, wish for our yard a plague of peacocks
with wide-eyed tails on permanent display.
                  Because of fear like this,

beautiful babies are given
ugly names. Women's faces smudged with ash. A bride veiled, a chuppah
hung as cloth bower against demonic assault. *Kina hora*, "no evil eye,"
tacked to the end of every shtetl compliment. Or, if far from the old
country, where *kina hora* twists the tongue, they say instead: *Don't give me
a canary*—in the coal mine of fate, such brightness is a provocation
begging to be broken.
In Italian, they call it
malocchio, in Spanish *el ojo*, simply "the eye," but in Yiddish, my grandmother
calls it, *git-oyg*, "the good eye"—a bubbe's pump-fake against disaster.

Like tonight, when the room's air has set like amber around our sounds
of pleasure, when you rest your face on my chest and say, *Thank you
for one of the best days of my life*. I kiss your forehead and say, *Yes, you're welcome*,
adding in my head, *for a terrible day. Pu-pu-pu. May it never be repeated.*

V.

We die and are put into the earth forever.
We should insist while there is still time.

—Jack Gilbert

Finding Something

After a shared run, walking a set of steep stairs: a shifting
in her thigh, deep in the belly of the muscle. I rub and
rub, trying to work the knot out—
                              as the one who urged her into her body,
I feel responsible for her pain. But, weeks later, the MRI names
its true name: a tumor, close
to the bone.

              Here we are
at this beginning after how many
beginnings passed and passed by, and now
this powder keg, this plague
                    perhaps
already strangling her bones, perhaps
ending her from the inside.
I listen to what she needs
to say, willing to discuss everything
except the possibility of her dying. There are
doctors to call, appointments to keep.

    Besides. The sun has lived
barely half its life. There's time.
                          I mean, it's taken
    half of mine to learn the only way
    to make anything matter
                    is to have her there

to witness it. There's time. We know
                              nothing
                       yet.
              There's time.

       Tell me there is.

In the Days Between Detection and Diagnosis

Ibershrekn mir, Got, ober strof mir nisht.
Scare me, God, but don't punish me.
—Yiddish Proverb

∞

What if this ultrasound
of my wife,

which shows
this something

growing
inside her, this mass

punctuating
the undulation

of her thigh,
is the closest

we come
to birth, this tumor

the most
her body conceives?

∞

Just down the street, I drop
her at the cancer center,
park, and minutes later, find her

near tears in the waiting room, trying not
to stare at a man with limbs lumpy as a scarecrow's,
tubes crawling his face. Alone,

I'd entered past a woman our age with one
pant leg cuffed to where her foot and ankle
should have been, then stepped into an elevator

where a bald man avoided contagion
by using his elbow. Hitting three floors
at once, he apologized and laughed—suddenly

handsome beneath skin so tight and translucent
I wanted to peel it back to
the real face beneath, the healthy one

he used to have. Still waiting, we keep
our eyes to the floor. I take her hand.
Who knows what she saw to get here.

∞

Taking her history—that strange
marauder's phrase—the nurse
is confused by "lumpectomy"
and needs help spelling

"benign." *Guess you don't*
type that much here, my wife
jokes. *No,* the nurse says
without smiling, *I don't.*

The resident with a cowlick
and cowboy boots palpates
her thigh like a boy
feeling up his first girl—

half-feeling, half-listening
for a father's heavy tread
on the stairs. The doctor,
when he finally enters,

talks too fast, breathes
three options, then says,
So what do you want to do?

∞

I want to take her as far
from this hospital
as I can. Anchor her

cheek to the steady
cadence of my chest
and live inside

the weekend, with its no
appointments, its no news.
Sweet stasis of Sunday,

our island
of unknowing.
My dread so dark

and heavy it's worth
delaying
any possible light.

∞

We drive hours south in search
of better care. Between appointments, after days
of rain, every step I run is a slickness threatening
skid, every step lichen and leaf rot. We retreat

inside the Rothko Chapel, its paintings lit
by what the sky provides. They change
as the weather does, as the day ticks down.

In the hospital, patients starting chemo are
identifiable by only a white bracelet. Later,
after closely dosed poison shears them
of shielding hair or beard, makes tallow
of their skin, makes their pulses flicker
dimly, no bracelets are needed.
                                        Here,
a muted constellation of these women
in head scarves, an array of faulty, defiant lamps.
I kiss the back of my wife's neck, its sun
and sweat the brightest shade
in the room,
                    then go sit closer to a canvas
to cry alone. When I turn, she is watching
my shoulders. She dips her head,
walks outside.

∞

I write of my love for her and never
come close to naming it. So what word
can claim God? False idols, crude cages:
within words, God is electricity
bucking in a bad breaker.

Instead, *via negativa*: just as it's
easier to sketch the space
around a tree than the intricacies
of the tree itself, God is described by
what God is not.
And what a relief, the open air
sanctuaries of apophatic prayer—
away from speech; the reprieve
of unsaying. Of clearing a space
in which God
can appear:

    Not of creation, God is not
    divisible. *Literally God is*
    not, because God
    transcends being. Enough

bricks of negation and we can babble
a tower tall enough to make
not a prison, not a house, but an instrument
through which Shekinah, the presence

of God, can sound.
                              I cannot say
what I believe. But I am listening.

∞

In my first real stillness in weeks, I begin
with negation: a prayer of *no*, of *not yet*, of all
the things I cannot bear.
                    Then simply,

    please.

                    Which binds this to how many
moments of spontaneous devastation:
the inhalation as I began our vows, the last mile
of my first marathon, the night I stood
on that ice field and lost track
of my edges.
                    Moments the world broke
through, or moreso, when what barricades me
from the world was broken, a small window
opened,
            like this single painting
on the entrance wall: a massive
black rectangle framed in maroon. A window of
darkness, into deeper darkness. No real promise
of eventual light. Only an opening, which
will have to do:

Please, you cold slate tiles. Please,
heavy benches with your clear shellac. Baffled
skylight letting the light in, letting my words
out; please, don't take her from me.

∞

She comes home with a milagro of a leg:
on a thin chain, bronze thigh to bronze foot tapping
her sternum. Meant to focus a saint's attention

on a supplicant's particular need, these amulets
hang from altars thick as a keymaker's wall
of blanks—symbols bristling with potential

entrance, though not yet capable of opening
even a single door. What would you do if you knew
you were going to die today? When death comes

it's always today. Yet when, in our bed, she moves
above me, that charm swings through the dark
and against the bottom of my chin, against my chest,

it chimes. Small miracle. Small
sweet signal through the silence that is this waiting.

When My Job Is to Wait

The stained glass is backlit to give the illusion
of a window, to simulate sunlight
instead of a bare bulb and a wall. No one
is fooled. Is anywhere more desperate
than a hospital chapel?
                              Pews crowd the low
altar. Two shivering animals, my hands
huddle into each other, wring themselves red.
A woman on a kneeler presses
her hands together and then to her face. Makes the sign
of the cross. Leaves without looking at me.
For whom did that kneeling woman pray?
        If I am bypassed by tragedy,
                    will it knock on her door instead?

A distant tolling:
my wife's wedding band on my right hand,
sparking against my own.
Wringing grief, ringing grief, relief
only when it's back on her finger.

Between the Kingdoms of The Sick and The Well

Illness is the night-side of life.
　　　　—Susan Sontag

Wherever the world's steepest bridge, can you picture us there?—
on the upward slog, on bikes heavy as cinderblocks, working
just to stay in place. The cyclists around us numerous

and varied as insects in the airstream: old men riding
children's bicycles, shaggy-haired hipsters on tricked-out fixies,
suits on commute-ready collapsibles. By night, though,

still pedaling, we are depersoned, visible
only for the light we emit, for the flash of our anti-crash
talismans. See it from afar: Between dark rush

of river and empty open of sky, the path
is a fragile filament and each of us a bead
of slow-moving light, seeking a return to shore.

(We call and call and call the hospital and finally hear:
Benign! We have the nurse repeat it twice to be sure.) Joy frees us
over and past the span's middle, movement going

from effort to effortless to inevitable. Yet even with this
speed, we are shadow-companioned, unable to forget
the reminders such darkness brings: Instead of sources

of any lasting light, our bodies are only obstructions (brief)
between radiance and the ground it seeks. Who knows which kingdom
we're ultimately heading toward? Yet we continue, urging

each other on, gamely splashing through puddles
of lamplight, chased by the shades of us even
as we race them, losing to ourselves every time.

Motion Artifact

Pre-op, we rocket through her thigh as rendered
by the MRI. In the haloed static
of muscle and skin, her femur in cross-section

is an old-fashioned keyhole; her tumor,
a dark fist. There's a faint blur; the doctor points, *That's
artifact motion, where you twitched a bit.*

Yet now that we know
   the tumor is benign,
      have errors ever sounded so beautiful?

        Gibbs Ringing, Magic Angle, Offset Ghost
  or,
       Once upon a time in New York,
         I went with the wrong woman to the right bar
         and met my wife.

Who wants a textbook image anyway, that grainy
imitation shorn of natural flow and twitch?

If an *artifact* is an object made
by art, and an *image artifact* the record
of what ripples out of that making, then

all that matters most of me is image artifact
of my hand resting in that bar beside hers.
Our lives an assemblage of such faint blurs

on the filmstrip. One thing I know for sure: the possibility
of losing her demanded from me everything
but complacency. Errors not mistakes, but records

of how we go from art
to the messy wonder of living.

VI.

We needed nothing then except each other,
     and that we needed all the time.

    —Maggie Anderson

Nevertheless

This time is sacred for the good or bad
it could become, but isn't yet. For the phone
that doesn't ring, but might.
     Ma nishtana ha-laila
    ha-zeh mi-kol ha-leilot?
      Why is this night
    different than all other nights?
      It's not. Only more
visible. More clearly the cusp each night is—

                                     cancer, one step
off the wrong curb, one moment when the heart forgets
to keep time. But such questions are essential.
During Passover, they enable the mitzvah of telling
the story that takes us from slavery
                            to freedom.
Even when celebrating alone, we are instructed
to ask ourselves these questions, to become
both the teller and the other
to whom the story is told:
   And on the night of the tenth plague,
   Israelites were instructed to sacrifice a lamb
   and mark with its blood their doorways
    so that the Angel of Death
    might pass over.
      Then we eat bitter
herbs to commemorate the pain
of those not passed by.

Why others, though,
and not us?
        I know nothing
that makes us worthy
of such consideration. And sometimes questions
are all I have left. Like what else is there
except to move forward?
                We found
our new home while her tumor
still nestled in bed between us—benign
but imperative reminder. We married
our books, packed and hauled,
walked our new rooms in wonder. And in hope
some trace remained, I ran my hands
along every doorway we entered.

The First Rule of Rock Tumbling
Is Rocks Must Be of Similar Hardness

Naked on the front porch, the moon unfurling
its light as though for a picnic, our yard is silver
and set for feasting.

               When we married, I
was all elbows and angles, with one pace, which
was my pace, which was fast

forward. She was all cushion and curve, considerable
sharpness shivved inside a pillow; deliberate
thinker, decision circler, all around

slow goer. Despite this, we loved hard enough
to want the other always at our side.
So, where others reminisce

of their early honeymoon years, ours were more
rock tumbler, more slurry and coarse grind,
two roughs bashing together until our edges wore

not smooth exactly but worn
into each other—gear-tight, cog in cog, turning
our shared hours.
               Like this hour on this night,

when I stand between the moon and her
so she wears the light
like an unzipped jumpsuit: shoulders plated,

nipples burnished, outer thighs striped bright.
At her center, my shadow, that tailor-made
eclipse, a darkness exactly my size—though

we could easily change places, and have,
and will. She steps (sides-lit),
I step (backlit), to match

our shaded places. And only once we're
fit like this, dark to dark, are we once more bound
                by the light we each carry.

Because You Waited for Me to Fly Your First Kite

                         Let our love be this clutch
of dogs off-leash: the preen and posture, snort
and snuffle, of saying, *I smell you*
and, therefore, know you. The rolling
on the backs and baring of the bellies.
And the tails! An exaltation of metronomes,
                         keeping time for their joy.

        If this summer is a body,
                         let me be its tongue.
Tasting the green tang of the spittlebug nests
foaming the oat grass, the iron of this
good dirt. A tongue to lick the salt
from your upper lip, the rosary of sweat
risen on your chest. A tongue to tap
the top teeth and suck back like a wave
whose tide rolls out through lips pursed
as though for a kiss.
                Listen
                again: *Thank you.*

        As in, please,
                let me be this kite
lifting from your hands—ruffled nylon paradise
bird, with its taut spine and cross spar, the pop
of its ripstop sails, snap of its translucent tails.

                                        Give me
the grand view: white water and mountains; but mostly

of you—head thrown back, face to the sun, holding
my traceline: tethered to you,
always, responding to the slightest
tick of your fingertips. Let me be a kite that trusts itself
to the sky.
        Yes, gravity is inevitable
     as death. But why let that desecrate
              even a moment of this flight?

On Our Nightly Walk, She Takes My Hand

Across the dark street, the dance studio
is a brilliant lamp, a Cornell box

set to music and motion: girls hold each other
in swaying *pas de deux*, a phrase

first translated for me as *piece of God*.
That's wrong, of course,

but not entirely. For what is it to move in time
with another, to acknowledge and learn

a body beside your own—the dancing apart
and the final coming back

together—what is this if not
                    some kind of grace,

some human-sized serving of God?

Notes

The initial epigraph is from Rainer Maria Rilke's *Letters to a Young Poet* (trans. M.D. Herter Norton).

Section I's epigraph is from Larry Levis's "My Story in a Late Style of Fire."

Section II's epigraph is from Alain de Botton's *On Love*.

"And That's How I Almost Died of Foolishness in Beautiful Florida" takes its title from a line in Mary Oliver's "Alligator Poem."

Section III's epigraph is from Jorie Graham's "Salmon."

In "Post Op, Still Out of It, You Said, I Would," the italicized section is a quote from the third section of Adrienne Rich's "Twenty-One Love Poems."

"Postcards After the Fall" is for Pamela Jody Stewart.

"Who Needs Premarital Counseling When We Have Nightly Visits to the Doubt Couch?" is for Robert Alexander and Katie Mead.

"Elopement Epithalamium" is for Laure-Anne Bosselaar.

The title of "Between the Shoreline and the Sea" is a riff on a line from Leonard Cohen's "Hey, That's No Way to Say Goodbye."

The epigraph for "In the Grove of Self-Charging Trees" is from Stanley Kunitz's "Touch Me."

The title "Curly, My Tangler," is a phrase from Pablo Neruda's "Sonnet XIV," as is that poem's epigraph. The final section owes a debt to Charles Simic's ode "Breasts."

Section V's epigraph is from Jack Gilbert's "Tear It Down."

"Finding Something" borrows its title and theme from Jack Gilbert's poem of the same name.

In the section of "In the Days Between Detection and Diagnosis" that begins, "I write of my love for her," the italicized text is from a quote by 9th century theologian Johannes Scotus Eriugena: "We do not know what God is. God Himself does not know what He is because He is not anything. Literally God is not, because He transcends being."

"Between the Kingdoms of The Sick and The Well" derives both its title and epigraph from the beginning of Susan Sontag's remarkable essay, "Illness as Metaphor:" "Illness is the night-side of life, a more onerous citizenship. Everyone who is born holds dual citizenship, in the kingdom of the well and in the kingdom of the sick. Although we all prefer to use only the good passport, sooner or later each of us is obliged, at least for a spell, to identify ourselves as citizens of that other place."

"Motion Artifact:" In radiology, a motion artifact is anything present in an image not present in the original object; caused sometimes by error, sometimes by the body's natural movement when an X-ray or MRI is taken.

Section VI's epigraph is from Maggie Anderson's "My Father and Ezra Pound."

Acknowledgments

I would like to thank the editors and staff of the following publications, in which these poems first appeared, sometimes in different forms or with different titles:

32 Poems, About Place, Academy of American Poets' *Poem-a-Day, The Adroit Journal, Alaska Quarterly Review, Asheville Poetry Review, The Bellingham Review, Bennington Review, Beloit Poetry Journal, The Collagist, The Compass (UK), Copper Nickel, Crazyhorse, Emrys Journal, Greensboro Review, The Heartland Review, MĀNOA, Michigan Quarterly Review, The Missouri Review, Normal School, One, Pilgrimage, Rattle, San Pedro River Review, The Shallow Ends, Southern Humanities Review, SWWIM, THRUSH,* and *Washington Square Review*

"Postcards Braver Than I Could Be" first appeared as "In the Canyon III (False Starts)" in *Pelvis with Distance* (White Pine Press)

"Stridulation Sonnet" appeared as a broadside for Charlotte Lit's 4x4CLT Series (art by Renee Calder) and for Asheville Bookworks' Vandercooked Poetry Series (art by Gary Hawkins)

From the sequence "In the Days Between Detection and Diagnosis," the section that begins "I write of my love for her and never;" and "When My Job is to Wait" were reprinted in *The Orison Anthology, Vol. II.* (Orison Press)

"Primer" was reprinted in *Southern Ecology Anthology* (Yellow Flag Press)

"A Question to Ask Once the Honeymoon Is Over" was reprinted in *Disturb & Enrapture: A Decade of Sibling Rivalry Press Poetry* (Sibling Rivalry Press)

Many of these poems also appeared in the chapbook *In Whatever Light Left to Us* (Sibling Rivalry Press)

∞

In Hebrew, one of the ways to say "grateful" is *ahseeraht toda*, a phrase whose literal translation is "bound by thanks." Though writing is a solitary practice, getting a book into the world is an act of great collaboration. To each who helped me, more than can be listed here, I am bound to you by my gratitude.

When my first collection and my wife's second were published the same year, we spent nearly six months on the road, a tour that wouldn't have been possible without the welcome of friends. In their guest rooms, cabins, and fold-out couches, most of these poems found their beginnings: Elizabeth & Andrew Sebastian and David Rice, Robert Alexander & Katie Mead, Craig Teicher & Brenda Shaughnessy (and Cal & Simone), Kelly Barth & Lisa Grossman, Janlori Goldman & Katherine Franke, Michael Waters & Mihaela Moscaliuc (and Fabian), Pamela Jody Stewart, Elizabeth Bradfield & Lisa Sette, Mary Lou Mooney, Dennis Maloney & Elaine LaMattina, Laura Pritchett, Shelly Catterson & Marcelo Games, Paul Pascarella, Allegra Huston (and Rafa), Nicole & Richard Pollitt, and Tracey & Renny Burke.

For the masterclass that is *Beloit Poetry Journal* editorial weekends, my thanks to Melissa Crowe, Rachel Contreni Flynn, Juliette Guilmette, Leonore Hildebrandt, Kirun Kapur, and Lee Sharkey.

If these poems have improved from their early drafts, much of that is due to the generosity and wisdom of poets Danielle DeTiberus and Matthew Olzmann; to Melissa Crowe, for seeing me and my poems more clearly than I often do myself; to Nina LaCour, with your novelist's eye for narrative arc, as well as my Asheville writing group: Maggie Anderson, Rebekah Hewitt, Luke Hankins, Gary Hawkins, Eric Nelson, and Rachel Shopper. Love to Bryan Borland and Seth Pennington of Sibling Rivalry Press for helping first send these poems into the world. Laure-Anne Bosselaar, your unerring eyes and ears (and heart) are invaluable.

To my students, who continue to teach me long after we've left the classroom.

To my parents, whose marriage of more than four decades has fostered a belief in lasting love and commitment, and an understanding of the work such commitment entails.

To Martha Rhodes, for welcoming me into the Four Way family and for your astute and artful editing; to Ryan Murphy, for your eye for design; Clarissa Long, for ushering this book into the world; Bridget Bell, for your careful proofing, and the rest of the Four Way staff.

And, to Nickole Brown, my first and best reader, thank you for helping every one of these poems become a better version of the one I first wrote and for trusting me to share these moments as I experienced them.

Jessica Jacobs is the author of *Pelvis with Distance* (White Pine Press, 2015), a biography-in-poems of Georgia O'Keeffe, winner of the New Mexico Book Award in Poetry and a finalist for the Lambda Literary Award. Her chapbook *In Whatever Light Left to Us* was published by Sibling Rivalry Press in 2016. Her poetry, essays, and fiction have appeared in publications including *Orion, New England Review, The Missouri Review, Crazyhorse,* and the *Oxford American.* An avid long-distance runner, Jessica has worked as a rock climbing instructor, bartender, editor, and professor, and is now the Associate Editor of the *Beloit Poetry Journal.* She lives in Asheville, North Carolina, with her wife, the poet Nickole Brown.

Publication of this book was made possible by grants and donations. We are also grateful to those individuals who participated in our 2018 Build a Book Program. They are:

Anonymous (11), Sally Ball, Vincent Bell, Jan Bender-Zanoni, Kristina Bicher, Laurel Blossom, Adam Bohanon, Betsy Bonner, Mary Brancaccio, Lee Briccetti, Jane Martha Brox, Carla & Steven Carlson, Caroline Carlson, Stephanie Chang, Tina Chang, Liza Charlesworth, Andrea Cohen, Machi Davis, Marjorie Deninger, Patrick Donnelly, Charles Douthat, Emily Flitter, Lukas Fauset, Monica Ferrell, Jennifer Franklin, Helen Fremont & Donna Thagard, Robert Fuentes & Martha Webster, Ryan George, Panio Gianopoulos, Chuck Gillett, Lauri Grossman, Julia Guez, Naomi Guttman & Jonathan Mead, Steven Haas, Lori Hauser, Mary & John Heilner, Ricardo Hernandez, Deming Holleran, Nathaniel Hutner, Janet Jackson, Rebecca Kaiser Gibson, David Lee, Jen Levitt, Howard Levy, Owen Lewis, Sara London & Dean Albarelli, David Long, Katie Longofono, Cynthia Lowen, Ralph & Mary Ann Lowen, Jacquelyn Malone, Fred Marchant, Donna Masini, Catherine McArthur, Nathan McClain, Richard McCormick, Victoria McCoy, Britt Melewski, Kamilah Moon, Beth Morris, Rebecca Okrent, Gregory Pardlo, Veronica Patterson, Jill Pearlman, Marcia & Chris Pelletiere, Maya Pindyck, Megan Pinto, Taylor Pitts, Eileen Pollack, Barbara Preminger, Kevin Prufer, Vinode Ramgopal, Martha Rhodes, Peter & Jill Schireson, Jason Schneiderman, Jane Scovel, Andrew Seligsohn & Martina Anderson, Soraya Shalforoosh, James Snyder & Krista Fragos, Ann St. Claire, Alice St. Claire-Long, Dorothy Tapper Goldman, Robin Taylor, Marjorie & Lew Tesser, Boris Thomas, Judith Thurman, Susan Walton, Calvin Wei, Bill Wenthe, Allison Benis White, Elizabeth Whittlesey, Rachel Wolff, Hao Wu, Anton Yakovlev, and Leah Zander.